Original title:
Roots of Resilience

Copyright © 2025 Creative Arts Management OÜ
All rights reserved.

Author: Colin Leclair
ISBN HARDBACK: 978-1-80567-452-8
ISBN PAPERBACK: 978-1-80567-751-2

The Tapestry of Survival

In a garden of socks, I found my lost shoe,
A dandelion's heart, still chasing the blue.
Butterflies gossip, while ants plan their schemes,
Life's a circus, bursting with whimsical dreams.

We juggle our failures, like fruit at a fair,
A pie made of troubles, we bake with a flair.
Potholes like puddles, we hop with delight,
Every bump in the road adds to our flight.

From Ashes, New Growth

A phoenix in pajamas, she snoozes and sighs,
While past mistakes roast marshmallows on skies.
We dance on the rubble, in shoes made of dust,
Spinning tales of triumph, with giggles and gusts.

Who knew that the ashes could serve us so well?
They sprinkle our cupcakes, with stories to tell.
Sprouts from the silly, and burps from the wise,
In the fumes of our failures, the sweetness does rise.

Branches That Bend

A tree with a bow tie, so sharp and so spry,
Rolls laughter like marbles, under a wide sky.
With branches that wiggle, they tickle the breeze,
Flexibility's big when it comes to the knees.

Who needs a straight path? Curves keep us fun,
We dance through the storms, while everyone runs.
A limbo of life where we shake off the grime,
We're brunch at a buffet, enduring through time.

When Winds Collide

Two breezes in combat, with hats on their heads,
They wrestle through gardens, and tumble from threads.
A twirl of confusion, a whirl of surprise,
Life's like a dance floor, with whimsy in highs.

When gusts meet the wiggles, the giggle is baked,
We're pizza with toppings, and never forsaken.
Each tussle with trouble, a carnival ride,
In the chaos of laughter, we bounce with pride.

Luminescence Amidst Darkness

When life throws you shadows, just laugh out loud,
Dance in the moonlight, join the rowdy crowd.
A tickle of starlight on your silly nose,
Makes giggles bloom like a garden of prose.

In tangled up troubles, find the punchline there,
Jokes sprout like daisies, floating in the air.
Bring on the bloopers, embrace every fall,
A chuckle is brighter than a neon ball.

Stories Carved in Time

In a world of mishaps, oh what a story,
Tripping on dreams, but never in worry.
Each clumsy moment, a giggle in waiting,
Life's frosty mistakes? They're all worth celebrating.

From blunders and fumbles, new tales arise,
A slip on a banana? Just see the surprise!
With every misstep, a legacy's penned,
In laughter we flourish, on humor we depend.

Undeterred by the Night

When darkness creeps in, don't slip on a shoe,
Wear mismatched socks, and make that a view.
With a wink and a grin, dance under the stars,
Who needs all the answers, when joy is our car?

The night hums a tune, but it can't steal our light,
We'll juggle our worries, till they take flight.
Sprinkling laughter like confetti in air,
For every scare, there's a giggle to spare.

Blossoms from Burdens

With burdens like backpacks, we stagger and sway,
But add a few giggles, and lighten the way.
Plant smiles like daisies in the soil of our hearts,
In the garden of life, humor's where it starts.

So let's trip on our dreams, with flair and a cheer,
Each stumble a solo, the laughter is near.
From struggles we bloom, like weeds in a patch,
In the landscape of joy, they make the best match.

Beneath the Surface

In the soil, the gnomes dig deep,
They whisper secrets, never sleep.
With garden tools, they waltz and sway,
Mixing comedy with their clay.

Earthworms laugh, they call the tune,
While daisies dance beneath the moon.
Gnarled roots stretch and twist around,
Trading jokes like clowns, profound.

The Strength Within

A tiny seed, so small and meek,
Cracks its shell, it starts to peak.
With a giggle, it bursts with pride,
In good humor, it won't hide.

Soil provides, with hugs so tight,
Encouraging growth day and night.
A bravado built, strong and tall,
As leaves grow wide, it smiles for all.

Unyielding Spirits

The cactus stands with arms stretched wide,
In the desert, it takes its stride.
Joking with sun, it grins real bright,
Sipping water, what a sight!

Even in drought, it doesn't fret,
With playful puns, it's quite the pet.
Amidst the thorns, it finds delight,
Spreading laughter, day and night.

Echoes of Endurance

Beneath the bark, the trees all chuckle,
As squirrels scurry, they never buckle.
With each gust, they sway and quake,
    Sharing stories of every shake.

Through storms and winds, they laugh and groan,
    In solidarity, they've shown.
    In every ring, a tale unfolds,
    Of jocular strength that never folds.

Fertile Ground

In a garden of laughter, we plant our dreams,
With weeds of worry, or so it seems.
Yet deep in the dirt, we chuckle and play,
Nature's the joker, making us sway.

A plant that knows jokes will surely survive,
Tickled by rain, it dances and dives.
With sunshine for giggles and rain for a shout,
We grow with a grin, that's what it's about!

Fragile Heart

When my heart wears pajamas, and feels oh so light,
I dance with my fears, what a comical sight!
For every giggle, there's a teeny-tiny crack,
But oh, how I twirl, no looking back!

I trip on my hopes, yet spring up with cheer,
Cracking jokes with my shadows that linger near.
With glittery band-aids on every small bruise,
I laugh at my stumbles, it's hard to lose!

Seeds of Strength

Little seeds tell tales, when buried they giggle,
Poking their heads just to show their riddle.
For the soil might chuckle, 'Go on, take a peek,'
It's all in the bounce, not just the technique!

Each sprout bears a grin, as it stretches wide,
Hoping to tickle the clouds up high.
For even the tallest, with roots underground,
Can't help but chuckle at what they have found!

The Embrace of Struggles

Oh, struggles are cuddly, like puppies in rain,
They jump on our backs, but we smile through pain.
With snickers for effort, we embrace the mess,
In the comedy show, we're all just the best!

Wrestling with woes that jump and that tease,
Each tumble and trip, just another breeze.
With humorous hearts, we tango with strife,
Finding the punchline - it's just how we life!

Rising from the Ruins

Out of the rubble, we pop up with flair,
Like cheeky cartoons, we bounce everywhere.
Through silliness and smiles, we conquer the dust,
Resilience is funny, a must-have, we trust!

When life gives a mess, we juggle with glee,
Unicycling clowns in our own jubilee.
So here's to the laughs, through thick and through thin,
Together we rise, let the fun begin!

Anchors in the Storm

When winds howl loud, pants fly low,
We dance like crazy, don't you know?
In puddles we leap, with smiles aglow,
Lost socks find homes, in a wild show.

Umbrellas flip like acrobats high,
We giggle as raindrops zoom by.
In chaos, we find our quirkiest ways,
Like chickens on stilts, we'll sway and play.

The ship may creak, the sails may droop,
But we're all aboard for the laughter troop.
Throw in some snacks, a comfy seat,
Even a storm can't beat our beat!

With hearts as anchors, we'll brave the tide,
In life's wet circus, we'll always ride.
With a wink and a grin, we hop and squirm,
After the storm, we'll bake up a firm.

Flourish from the Fractures

In the garden of mishaps, blooms sprout wide,
With twirls and tumbles, we'll take them in stride.
A flat tire's just a chance to dance,
We turn our flops into a grand prance.

The cake fell down, oh what a sight,
But hey! Let's decorate it with a giggle fight.
Pour in the sprinkles, let the laughter rise,
A floppy dessert can still win the prize!

When glasses break, we'll make some art,
Our crafty ideas will set us apart.
With glue and glitter, we'll mend the scene,
Who knew that a mishap could be so keen?

So here's to the fumbles that spice our days,
We stumble and tumble, then graph our ways.
In every fracture, there's fun to find,
With laughter as soil, we're one of a kind!

Resilient Whispers

In the chatter of chaos, we giggle and peek,
The world turns clumsy, adopting its cheek.
A toddler's tantrum? A grand performance!
In the sighs of the universe, we find our balance.

Tiny whispers of hilarity grow,
Like ants on a picnic, they steal the show.
With overcooked noodles that dance on the floor,
We laugh 'til we cry, then cry for more!

The toast may be burnt, but we've got the jam,
For every hiccup, we add "Yes, we can!"
Mix in a joke, a pun or two,
In the heart of the fuss, humor breaks through.

So let's whisper sweet nothings to each grouchy cloud,
Laugh at the grumbles, shout joyfully loud.
For in these soft moments, resilience will bloom,
With giggles as petals, we'll fill up the room.

Against the Grain

When plans unravel in delightful twist,
We'll craft new journeys, tripping in mist.
Like clumsy penguins on an ice spree,
Life's odd little moments, so wild and free!

Special deliveries from the weird and wacky,
Our life's recipe is truly snappy.
We toss the rules like confetti confound,
Stay quirky and wild, let spontaneity abound!

With socks of mismatches and hair of zest,
We strut to our own tune, we're truly the best.
Even in chaos, we rise from the grain,
In every odd turn, we'll dance through the pain.

So here's to the splatters, the blunders we make,
To celebrate life's humor, for laughter's own sake.
With each little wobble, may joy always reign,
In our canvas of chaos, let's sparkle again!

Breath of the Unbroken

When life throws pies right at your face,
Just laugh it off, it's part of the race.
With whipped cream smiles, we dance on through,
Who knew that slipping had such a good view?

When storms are brewing, and you can't find your coat,
Just grab a rubber duck and float like a boat.
Splashes of joy amidst the wild winds,
Sailing through chaos, that's how fun begins!

Journey of the Undeterred

Stumbling on rocks, with shoes tied in knots,
We imagine ourselves as graceful robots.
Every trip and fall is a dance of delight,
Who needs a map when you've got sheer fright?

We jog with clumsiness, a glorious fight,
Turning each mishap into pure delight.
With laughter as fuel and joy in our step,
The path may be bumpy, but we're never inept.

Flourishing Under Pressure

Under pressure, we pop like popcorn—
Silly and loud, we laugh until dawn.
In the heat of the moment, can't find our way,
Yet somehow we bloom like it's spring every day.

With every squashed bug and spilled cup of tea,
We jump into chaos, as happy as can be.
In the kitchen of life, we mix up the fun,
Who needs a recipe? We're already spun!

The Canvas of Courage

With paint on our faces and splatters in hair,
We create a masterpiece with life's little flare.
Each blunder a brushstroke, each fall a fine line,
The canvas of courage sparkles—divine!

We trip over colors, we step on our toes,
But laughter is vibrant, as everyone knows.
In this gallery of giggles, we proudly display,
That messy can also be joyous and gay!

Rising from Ashes

From the ashes I rise, oh what a sight,
Like a phoenix in pajamas, ready to take flight.
I trip over my dreams, as they scatter around,
But laughing's the magic that keeps me unbound.

In a world full of quirks, I dance on my toes,
With mismatched socks and an awkward pose.
Each misstep is gold, a treasure to find,
With every stumble, a giggle unwind.

Through the mess and the mayhem, I'll fight my way clear,
Wearing a crown made of spoons, shining with cheer.
With a wink and a nudge, I conquer my fears,
As I juggle my hopes while throwing back beers.

So raise up your glasses, let laughter resound,
For in jest, we find strength in the chaos around.
The ashes, they whisper, "You're never alone!"
Just remember to laugh; this life's a sitcom!

The Silent Courage

In shadows I linger, with valor concealed,
Like a ninja on tiptoes, my fate is revealed.
With a chuckle in silence, I conquer the scene,
Wearing pajamas in public—oh, ain't it a dream?

With each gulp of courage, I sip from my cup,
A mixture of giggles, with wisdom thrown up.
I may not be loud; my bravery's sly,
Like a cat in a hat, with a twinkle in eye.

Some folks will shout, while I'm on the low,
Crafting my plan like a sneaky-show pro.
With a nudge and a wink, I softly proceed,
Like a turtle in heels, I'll grow with great speed.

So here's to the quiet, the giggles they stow,
With courage in whispers, we let our light glow.
In the game of life, it's the subtle sparks,
That light up the shadows, leaving their marks.

Echoes in the Wind

The wind carries laughter, like a mischievous tune,
In a dance with the daisies beneath the bright moon.
Each whisper a chuckle, each gust a good cheer,
As I twirl in the meadows, ditching all fear.

With a basket of wishes, I gather them tight,
Sprinkling them freely where hope takes flight.
Like a jester in bloom, I'm dressed for the jest,
With each gust of fortune, I'm feeling the best.

The echoes remind me of moments gone by,
When I slipped on a pond and let out a cry.
Yet the laughter that follows is sweeter than gold,
In the banquet of life, it's the stories retold.

So I'll laugh with abandon, let joy take the wheel,
For the wind carries whispers we all can feel.
In the dance of the leaves, we find a new way,
To embrace every moment, come what may!

Shielding the Heart

With a shield made of giggles, I battle the day,
In bubble wrap armor, I won't fade away.
Laughter's my sword; it cuts through the gloom,
As I dance through the chaos, making room.

Those frowns on the faces? They're nothing but jest,
I'll tickle the troubles and put them to rest.
Underneath my umbrella of humor so bright,
I'll shield off the worries with all of my might.

Like a circus on wheels, my heart starts to race,
With each laugh that erupts, I find my own space.
Through the storms and the shenanigans, I stay afloat,
Riding waves of hilarity, on a bright, silly boat.

So here's to the laughter, our powerful art,
A shield that protects and brightens the heart.
In a world full of bonkers, I won't fall apart,
For laughter's the armor; come on, play your part!

Silent Warriors

In pajamas, they stand tall,
Mismatched socks, they conquer all.
With snacks held high, they charge ahead,
Kitchen battles fought instead!

With laughter loud, they slay the day,
Through laundry piles, they make their way.
With every spill, they find a cheer,
Messy warriors, have no fear!

They wield a broom like a mighty sword,
Each crumb a foe, they can't afford.
In silence, they dance, a crazy jig,
Champions of chaos, oh so big!

So raise a toast, to those at home,
In funny fights, they surely roam.
For every stumble, every pratfall,
We cheer them on, the best of all!

Threads of Tenacity

With threadbare jeans and lots of flair,
They stitch a life, without a care.
Each button lost, a tale to tell,
Of fashion faux pas, oh so swell!

In weekends spent in DIY bliss,
With saws and glue, it's hit or miss.
For every project that goes awry,
A masterpiece forms, oh me, oh my!

With tape on hands, they craft their fate,
Their greatest tools? A little wait.
For laughter keeps the spirits bright,
As they take flight, in crafty height!

The world would spin, in dull and gray,
Without the threads of funny play.
So let's applaud, their mishaps bold,
In the fabric of life, they shine like gold!

In the Quiet Aftermath

When silence falls, the chaos fades,
In piles of toys, true peace invades.
They tiptoe round, like stealthy spies,
In search of snacks, with hopeful eyes.

The dog snickers, the cat rolls wide,
As humans nap, they plot and bide.
For every blanket fort they make,
A sushi roll, just might awake!

In aftermath, the mess retreats,
With shrieks of joy, like tasty treats.
They savor laughter, as crumbs resound,
In peace they find the funny ground!

So come what may, in quiet bliss,
These folks wear smiles with every twist.
In aftermath, the joy won't cease,
For laughter's the ultimate peace!

Embracing the Unknown

With blindfolds on, they take the leap,
Into the depths, where laughter's heap.
With every stumble, there's a grin,
As they embrace the chaos within.

In kitchens wild, they mix and blend,
Oh what a dish, would they recommend?
With mystery meals, they cheer in style,
Cooking's an art, that's worthwhile!

Each corner turned, a quirky surprise,
Adventures await, in funny disguise.
With maps drawn wrong, but hearts so light,
They dance through life, finding delight!

So here's to fun, in paths unknown,
With every misstep, wisdom grown.
For life's a ride, where laughs abound,
In the dance of chaos, joy is found!

Unbreakable Ties

In the garden where the weeds play,
I dance with thorns, a light ballet.
Laughing at how they try to thrive,
  While I just wiggle to survive.

The chickens laugh and cluck away,
  As I trip over roots that sway.
My shoes are tangled in the mess,
  But I still strut, I must confess.

A squirrel jumps and steals my hat,
I chase him down, but where's he at?
I find my glasses on the ground,
With laughter echoing all around.

So here I stand, a comic sight,
With tangled legs and heart so bright.
In chaos, joy grows undeterred,
For laughter blooms in every word.

The Weight of Standing Tall

With every inch I reach for skies,
My back reminds me—oh, the lies!
I stretch my limbs like silly string,
And watch my neighbors laugh and sing.

The wind's a joker, tousles my hair,
I try to pose, but it's just unfair.
I sway and wobble, strike a pose,
While giggling kids say, 'There she goes!'

The trees around me shake their heads,
As I attempt to balance on threads.
I promise them I'll grow quite stout,
Just wait until I figure out!

But here I stand, with silly grace,
Chasing laughter all over the place.
For when I trip, though pride may fall,
It's better to laugh than not at all!

Cracked Earth, Flourishing Life

On dusty ground where laughter's rare,
A cactus blooms without a care.
'What's this? A party?' it declares,
While everyone else just glares and stares.

The cracks like rivers dance below,
Yet life bursts forth in funny show.
A lizard dons a funny hat,
And prances past a sleeping cat.

With cacti hats and laughter near,
They toss confetti made of cheer.
The earth may crack, but don't you frown,
For life finds ways to wear a crown.

So let's rejoice in every crack,
Even if it feels like a whack.
For out of humor, blooms so spry,
A little joy beneath the sky.

Buried Stories

Beneath the ground where secrets sleep,
Lie tales so funny, oh so deep.
A toe stubbed hard, a worm that slips,
Turned me into a dance of flips!

The gophers giggle, play their tunes,
While I dig deep under bright moons.
They whisper secrets, share their tricks,
I find a fortune in their licks.

With every shovel's playful toss,
I drop my sandwich, what a loss!
But find a treasure, old and cracked,
A memory wrapped, a joy unpacked.

So here's to stories held so tight,
In laughter's glow, they take their flight.
For every tale that goes unheard,
May sprout a giggle, a hearty word.

Rising Dreams

In the morning light, dreams take flight,
Like pancakes flipping, such a sight.
I dream of wealth, but not the stress,
Just fluffy clouds in a bright dress.

With every flounder of my day,
I learn to laugh and dance away.
'What's next?' I shout to passing ants,
They wave their tiny hands and prance.

With each misstep, I rise anew,
Creating dreams both bright and blue.
Like butterflies in a cake parade,
Turning clumsy moves to a grand charade.

So here's a toast to all who fail,
May our hearts rise beyond the pale.
For dreams are funny when they gleam,
And laughter's always part of the scheme.

Stronger Than Yesterday

Woke up this morning, felt like a champ,
Danced with my coffee, did a little stamp.
With every spill, I wore a grin,
For even splashes make a lively din.

The cat eyed my toast, decided to pounce,
I laughed as it leaped, doing a bounce.
No falling apart, just a little mess,
Life's quirks remind me it's all a jest.

Ran through the rain, a slip and a slide,
Laughter erupted; I took it in stride.
Each puddle's a challenge, a leap of delight,
Portal to fun, in the skies so bright.

Each stumble a laugh, like a comedy show,
I've got my own groove, just watch me go!
Stronger I stand, with my silly grace,
In this dance of mishaps, there's no better place.

Symphony of Resilience

Life plays a tune, with notes so bizarre,
Bouncing along like a clumsy guitar.
With each little hiccup, I join in the song,
Swinging my arms, it won't be long.

Cabbage on my head, that's fashion, they say,
Whirling in circles, in my own weird way.
Twirls and triumphant, I conquer the floor,
This offbeat parade, who could ask for more?

Donuts in hand, I juggle and spin,
Peanut butter splats; oh where to begin?
With laughter's percussion, the chaos is grand,
A joyful symphony, together we stand.

Even when life throws a custard pie,
I'll catch it with style, and give it a try.
Each mishap I face, I'll make it a jest,
In this quirky concert, I'm surely the best!

The Dance of Survival

In the kitchen I'm twirling, a dish in my hand,
Flour on my nose, ah, isn't life grand?
The dog joins the waltz, he's got some good moves,
Together we jiggle, breaking all grooves.

Tripped on a rug, landed right on the floor,
The cat gave a chuckle, 'Oh, not that once more!'
Stumbled through life, oh what a show,
With every mishap, my spirit will glow.

Dance party of one, with socks full of funk,
Shimmies and shakes, no time to be junk.
The vacuum's my partner, we're spinning in place,
In this offbeat ballet, I'll win any race.

Survival's a dance, with the world as my stage,
Embracing the chaos, I'll never disengage.
Each pratfall I take becomes a grand swirl,
In this jolly life, let my laughter unfurl.

Fractals of Strength

Wiggly and wobbly, that's how I stand,
Juggling my snacks with a sprinkle of sand.
Each crumb gets a giggle, a tasty delight,
Sprinkling joy like stars in the night.

Life's puzzle pieces, all over the floor,
I trip on my dreams, but come back for more.
With socks that don't match, and hair full of flair,
I twirl through the chaos, without any care.

Wrestling my worries, these curls like to bounce,
Every little problem, I teach it to flounce.
In a whirlwind of laughter, I make my own way,
Finding strength in the silly, come what may.

So here's to the bumbles, the laughs that we share,
In tangles of life, each mistake is a dare.
Within these odd fractals, like flowers that grow,
Is a patchwork of joy, in the ebb and the flow.

Through the Cracks

In the sidewalk, weeds do grin,
Dancing boldly in the din.
They don't mind the muddy shoe,
Laughing as they push on through.

A fence may try to block their way,
But they just giggle, 'Let's not play!'
With each crack, they see the light,
Wiggling roots, oh what a sight!

Who knew concrete felt this bold?
Weed adventures never old.
With every gust, they sway and twirl,
Nature's jokes, they swirl and whirl.

So when you trip, just take a peek,
Life's a garden, not oblique.
Embrace the cracks and let them cheer,
For joy sprouts out, my dear, my dear!

Seeds of Tenacity

A seed once said, 'I'll find my way!'
With sunlight dancing, all will play.
Through dirt and muck, they made a pact,
Their stubbornness was quite intact.

They faced the rain, the wind so bold,
With every drop, their laughter flowed.
'Oh look, a storm!' they chirped with glee,
Keep spinning 'round, it's wild and free!

They sprouted high and waved to bees,
Sipping sun and sipping breeze.
In the garden, they threw a party,
With petals bright, they danced all hearty!

So if you trip on life's quicksand,
Remember seeds, and join their band.
With giggles loud and roots so spry,
Together, we can touch the sky!

The Heart's Backbone

Deep inside, a laugh does bloom,
A hearty giggle fills the room.
When life feels heavy, just let loose,
Dance like your feet belong to moose!

A beat, a jive, a twist, a turn,
The heart's a dance floor, let it churn.
Even if you trip and fall,
Just roll around and have a ball!

With every stumble, chuckle near,
That's the joy we hold so dear.
For in the goofy, we do shine,
Our backbone's laughter intertwines!

So when the road feels steep and rough,
Keep on laughing, that's enough!
With wiggly hearts and ticklish bones,
We build our strength in silly tones!

In the Eye of Adversity

A squirrel once faced a fierce storm,
With clumsy leaps, he dared to swarm.
He chattered loud, like a trusty friend,
'Stay strong, my pals, let's just pretend!'

With acorns flying all around,
He took a brave and silly bound.
'If I don't laugh, I might just drown,'
With every jump, he spun around!

The tree branches shook, a wiggly fight,
But he just giggled, 'What a sight!'
In all the chaos, joy is found,
In every leaf that spins around.

So when the winds of change do how–
Remember the squirrel and take a bow!
With laughter bright and hearts so free,
We'll float together, just you and me!

Wings of the Undaunted

When life throws pies, just duck and weave,
With laughter loud, we learn to grieve.
A slip, a slide, a funny fall,
Yet here we are, we stand up tall.

Like ducks in rain, we waddle through,
Finding joy in every hue.
With giggles bright, we paint the skies,
Who knew we'd soar, rather than cry?

When storms approach, we dance and spin,
Making faces, laughing with kin.
We'll take our spills, a sight to behold,
In this circus life, we strike gold.

So if you stumble, just smile wide,
We're all just clowns on this wild ride.
With hearts so light, we flap our wings,
And through the chaos, oh how it sings!

Heartbeats of Hope

With every thump, a chuckle starts,
In life's weird game, we play our parts.
A heartbeat drum, a wobbly beat,
We pull all pranks, but can't be beat!

When doubts arise like clowns at a fair,
We juggle dreams with skillful flair.
A tumble here, a slip right there,
Yet in the end, it's laughter we share.

With every setback, a joke we tell,
A funny face cast straight from hell.
Life's punchlines strike, we twist and bend,
Through every laugh, we learn to mend.

As hope dances, our spirits soar,
We chuckle louder, want more and more!
With every beat, the world's a stage,
In this wild comedy, we'll turn a page.

Strings of Tenacity

Grab your strings, it's time to play,
We'll stretch our minds in a wacky way.
With pokes and prods, we'll tie and knot,
In the game of life, it's all we've got.

Like elastic bands with a twist of fate,
We'll bounce back fast, we'll never wait.
Through silly gags, we swing around,
Unshaken, here, in laughter we're found.

In moments grim, our humor shines,
We'll slap a smile, make foolish designs.
Jokes strung together, giggles ignite,
Clinging to joy, our spirits take flight.

So pluck those strings, let laughter ring,
In this mad dance, we're kings and queens.
With hearty wit, we banter and tease,
In this circus act, we do as we please!

In the Midst of Fury

When tempests brew, we wear big hats,
And dance around like chubby cats.
With wobbling steps, we wade through strife,
Turning chaos into a funny life.

Our tempers flare, then bubble pop,
We giggle soft, then hear the plop.
Like a rubber chicken, we'll squawk and squeal,
In silly storms, we find our zeal.

In fury's face, we flash a grin,
With roller skates, let's just begin!
We glide through troubles, holding tight,
In this joyful mess, we find our light.

Through raucous laughter, we find our strength,
In every fumble, there's boundless length.
So here's to joy in darkest hours,
With funny bones, we bloom like flowers!

Tapestry of Trials

In the garden of chaos, we plant our dreams,
Water them daily with ice cream streams.
When storms come a-knocking, we dance in the rain,
With mismatched socks, we'll entertain the pain.

We juggle our troubles like oranges bright,
Wearing clown shoes that squeak, what a sight!
Each setback a twist in our silly parade,
We laugh at the mess, our fears start to fade.

A tapestry woven with threads made of cheer,
Winding through moments of laughter and fear.
When the world hands us lemons, we just make a pie,
Add a pinch of giggles, let the good times fly.

So here's to the journey with all its quirks,
Embracing our fumbles, the laughter it sparks.
For in every blunder, the fun's not a chore,
We'll dance to our trials, and open the door.

Whispers of Hope

In a world full of mishaps, we wear our best shoes,
Stumbling like toddlers, we refuse to lose.
With pockets of jellybeans, we skip down the street,
Adding giggles and grins to each day's heartbeat.

When shadows creep in like a ticklish breeze,
We tell them to shoo like pesky bees.
We'll paint silly faces on everyday woes,
And chuckle at life like a quirky old prose.

With every trip forward, we trip on our laces,
But laughter's the glue in our tangled up spaces.
We chase after sunbeams, we dance with the breeze,
Each whisper of hope is a tickle, a tease.

So let's toast to the laughter, the misses and hits,
The glow of resilience through hiccups and splits.
In a garden of humor, we bloom with a smile,
Turning frowns into giggles, let's linger awhile.

Foundations of Fortitude

We build our strongholds on sand and on jest,
With marshmallow bricks, we're trying our best.
When life hands us puzzles, we laugh at the ends,
Each piece is a giggle, our quirky best friends.

Like kittens in boxes, we pounce on our dreams,
Unraveling mishaps, or so it seems.
With butterflies dancing on hope's merry wings,
We craft our tomorrows from all funny things.

Each stumble a thrill, we embrace every fall,
Like juggling cats at a stand-up call.
Our foundations are silly, but sturdy and bright,
We'd rather be laughing than locked up in fright.

So here's to the laughter and all that it brings,
A fortress of fun made from whimsical strings.
With a wink and a grin, let's conquer each fray,
For the strength that we build is a comical play.

Grit and Grows

With grit in our pockets and smiles on our face,
We tumble through life at a ridiculous pace.
Like squirrels with backpacks, we gather our nuts,
While singing loud anthems that fit like our guts.

Each failure a flavor, a quirky dessert,
A sprinkle of chaos, a dash of the hurt.
When life gives us lemons, we squirt them with flair,
And sip lemonade while reciting a dare.

In this circus of life, we're the clowns with the might,
We juggle our struggles with all of our might.
With a wink and a wobble, we tackle the grind,
For every setback's a story, hilarious and kind.

So let's wear our capes, our duds filled with cheer,
With laughter our antidote, we've nothing to fear.
Together we flourish, like flowers that know,
That sometimes the path is just how we grow.

Mosaic of Survival

Once I tripped on a banana peel,
But I bounced right back with a squeal.
Life can be slippery, no doubt about,
But humor's my armor, there's no room for pout.

In the face of chaos, I dance and I spin,
Like a toddler who's just learned to grin.
Each stumble is just a step in disguise,
A slapstick reminder to laugh till I cry.

With every mishap, a tapestry grows,
Each twinkle of laughter, a thread that just glows.
I'm a mosaic of giggles, of blunders and glee,
Crafting a picture that's vibrant and free.

So, when life throws its curveballs my way,
I dodge and I weave, I refuse to dismay.
In the circus of living, I'm juggling my fate,
With a chuckle and wink, life's good; isn't it great?

Guiding Lights in the Dark

In the middle of night, my fridge starts to hum,
It's a beacon of hope when I feel kind of glum.
Pasta from yesterday, a warrior in arms,
With cheese as my shield, oh, it surely charms.

When the world feels like a game of charades,
I pull out some snacks and throw endless parades.
Dancing with chips, twirling with dip,
Even sour cream can learn a cool flip!

My bed's a fortress, my blanket a shield,
I summon the giggles, no battle to yield.
With laughter my lantern, I'll navigate through,
The dark's just a canvas for laughter's bright hue.

As stars tease the sky with celestial glee,
I'll waltz with the shadows, just watch me be free.
So here's to the brightness that laughter ignites,
In dark times we're silly, and that's what delights!

Strength Beneath the Surface

I'm like an iceberg, but I'm all silly glee,
What's hidden below? A big cup of tea!
With a dash of sass and a sprinkle of cheer,
I'll float through the chaos, let's give it a cheer!

Life's tossed me a few punches and kicks,
But I counter with witticisms, clever little tricks.
My strength's in the giggles, the silly mistakes,
And every joke told is a dance that I make.

When troubles erupt like a wild, yappy dog,
I'll tickle its tummy, no need for a fog.
With each little bark, I just join in the play,
Turning woes into laughter, that's how I stay.

Beneath all the blunders, there's courage galore,
Like a clam with a pearl, I'm filled to the core.
So if you need strength, come giggle along,
We'll find our resilience in dance and in song!

Echoes of Endurance

In the echo of laughter, I hear my own cheer,
Bouncing back quick when I'm gripped by my fear.
Life's not precision, it's more like a game,
Where I can wiggle and squirm – oh, how it's lame!

With every small slip, I invent a new style,
Trip like a cartoon, then bounce back with a smile.
My blunders are music, each fall is a note,
Together they create a resilience remote.

When rain clouds appear with a thunderous roar,
I grab my old umbrella and dance on the floor.
Each raindrop a rhythm, each puddle a stage,
We'll rock the storm out; let's break out the page.

So here's to the echoes that follow each jest,
In silliness hides all the strength we've expressed.
Together we chuckle as the world spins around,
In laughter, enduring, our joy will astound!

Unraveled Yet Whole

My socks are mismatched, that's quite a feat,
Yet they dance perfectly with two left feet.
My plants are wilting, not a single sprout,
But in their pot, they still hold a clout.

Grandma's stories are wild, like a runaway horse,
She once fought a dragon, and, of course,
She lost her shoe in a pie-making fight,
Yet we laugh, for her wisdom is always in sight.

A puzzle missing pieces, none can complete,
Yet we find joy in the search, oh so sweet.
Life's tangled like spaghetti tossed on a wall,
But each twist and turn is a laugh by us all.

With every fall, a slapstick show,
From tripping on air, to letting things go.
We're a mess, yet our laughter still holds,
In the chaos of life, true courage unfolds.

The Power of Quiet

In a world that's loud, I seek the hush,
Where thoughts can tumble and softly rush.
A garden growing in the still of the night,
Whispers of wisdom that take flight.

My neighbor's dog plays the trumpet quite proud,
But a quiet sneeze can make the heart loud.
In silence, we can share the silliest grin,
Like talking to magpies, spinning tales from within.

Mom says quiet is where ideas brew,
While the cat plots and ponders the silly things too.
In every still moment, we laugh at the sounds,
Life's goofy parade in the quiet surrounds.

So here's to stillness, weird and wild,
Where laughter blooms, untamed and styled.
In the power of calm, we find our sweet plot,
In the giggles of silence, we're gifted a lot.

Lemonade from Lemons

With life's sour fruit, I take a big sip,
Mix in some laughter, let giggles equip.
When life throws tartness, I dance in the rain,
For frowning just makes my cheeks hurt in vain.

Squeezing those lemons may make me all pucker,
But with sugar and laughs, I can freely chuckle.
A splash of mischief, a hint of cheer,
I brew up my drink, and it brings in good cheer.

I once tripped on lemons and found my own way,
Fell into laughter like I was on display.
From a zesty bouquet, I serve up delight,
In every sip, find the fun in the plight.

So cheers to the lemons, they've taught me so well,
To chuckle and dance as I weave my own spell.
With humor's sweet twist, I'll take on the task,
For life's just a blast when you're willing to bask.

Awakening the Hidden

In the depths of my closet, treasures align,
Old wigs and costumes, a goldmine divine.
With a tutu from disco and a cape from the 80s,
I dance in reflection, oh how the past wafties!

The dust bunnies giggle, as I start to sway,
To rhythms of memories that brighten the gray.
A topsy-turvy jig in my jammies, oh yes,
Unraveling laughter, amidst all the mess.

Finding lost treasures is quite the dare,
Like finding mismatched socks in thin air.
With every old trinket, a story unfolds,
In the attic of life, pure joy never molds.

So here's to the hidden, let's bring them to light,
With costumes and jokes, let's shine oh so bright.
Awakening humor from remnants of yore,
Each laugh is a treasure, let's open the door!

Voices of the Unseen

In the land of lost socks, they cheer,
Worn-out flip-flops, no need to fear.
With every misstep, they laugh aloud,
Invisible friends, so vivid, so proud.

They whisper secrets in fanciful jest,
Turning life's chaos into a grand fest.
Bumbling around with a comedic flair,
They dance on the edge of the wildest dare.

Laundry's a mystery, a puzzling game,
Each shirt, a story, all sound the same.
Crumbs in the couch act as treasure to find,
A quest of the quirky, surreal and kind.

From dust bunnies rising, they start a parade,
A conga of chaos, yet never dismayed.
In the clutter of life, their laughter's the key,
Voices of the unseen, alive and so free.

Anchored in Dreams

On a paper boat made of yesterday's plans,
Setting sail with my mismatched cans.
Glory to jellybeans, sparkled and bold,
Each gummy a dream that never grows old.

In the bathtub harbor, I navigate time,
With rubber duck captains, all in their prime.
The shampoo waves crash, a sudsy delight,
Sailing through galaxies, all day and night.

Spoons fly like seagulls, their mission quite clear,
Stirring up adventure, spreading good cheer.
The soap foam clouds wrap my worries away,
On this wobbly journey, I'm king for the day.

Anchored in daydreams, I'll drift and I'll laugh,
Here in my vessel, I'm captain and half.
With laughter as wind, I'll go where I please,
In fanciful waters, I dance with the breeze.

Mending with Grace

In the patchwork of life, we stitch up the tears,
With glitter and glue, we conquer our fears.
Snagged a small sweater, with yarn on the run,
Pulled threads into giggles; oh, what fun!

Needles prickle softly, in hues of delight,
Creating a quilt made of starry-night bites.
Each patch is a story, with laughter at heart,
Sewing together the chaos, we start.

Button's a brawler, a feisty old chap,
Hanging on tightly, giving life a slap.
With every mishap, we craft out of grace,
A tapestry woven with joy in this space.

Mending our hearts at the seams of the day,
A band of misfits, come out to play.
With threads of humour, we tailor our fate,
In the fabric of laughter, we'll happily wait.

Survival's Serenade

In the wild world of lunchboxes, we thrive,
Hiding old snacks where the ants dare to dive.
With apples that giggle and sandwiches sing,
Survival's a feast, oh, what joy it can bring!

Bentos like battleships, stacking all high,
Fruits in the cannon, aiming for the sky.
In the tangle of carrots, like soldiers they stand,
All ready to march, a delicious demand.

Soup spills like secrets, a pot of pure fun,
With noodles as strings, tying laughter as one.
Got pickles on trumpets, they sound out a cheer,
A symphony crafted from joy that's sincere.

In the chaos of kitchens, we whistle and sway,
Mixing up magic throughout every day.
With laughter as seasoning, we stir up the cheer,
In the song of our lives, we dance without fear.

Through the Weaving

In a world where socks go missing,
A dance begins, oh, what a listing!
Threads intertwine, laugh and tease,
While mismatched pairs bring us to our knees.

Crafters shout, 'Look, what I've spun!'
Yarns of chaos blending, just for fun.
With every stitch, a giggle escapes,
As we weave through life, with all of its shapes.

The loom hums soft tunes of cheer,
Knitting our stories, year after year.
Laughter wraps 'round like a cozy shawl,
Binding our hearts, we rise through it all.

So grab a hook, or maybe a string,
Join in the dance, let your heart sing!
For every twist, knot, or little fray,
We find our joy, come what may!

Threads of Fortitude

Woven with quirks and a dash of glee,
Life throws curveballs like it's one big spree.
Stitching laughter in every fraught seam,
Who knew survival could be such a dream?

With needles in hand, we poke and we prod,
Creating a fabric that's oddly flawed.
Patternless madness, yet oh so divine,
Each twist and turn makes us truly shine.

Hiccups in life? We'll just call them flair,
Turning mishaps into threads we can wear.
So let's salute our unplanned designs,
Crafting together, our spirits align!

In the great quilt of all who have tried,
Each patch tells a tale, some giggle, some cried.
So here's to our fabric, wild and free,
Life's artful tapestry, just wait and see!

Finding Light in the Cracks

In the garden of life where weeds might sprout,
We dig through the dirt, and we pull them out.
With spades made of laughter and hats of dreams,
We plant seeds of joy in jumbled seams.

Cracks in the pavement? Oh, what a score!
We find daisies dancing, beggars wanting more.
With sunshine so silly, it warms even the glares,
Those cracks become pathways—improbable stairs!

Every fumble and tumble, a reason to cheer,
Step on the paths, let go of the fear.
Puddles of laughter reflect in the day,
There's beauty in blunders guiding the way!

So let's sashay through the cracks in our stride,
Sprinkling joy as our compass and guide.
Every stumble just adds to our charm,
Finding brightness in life keeps us warm!

Spiral of Strength

Round and round in this whirl of a ride,
We spiral up high, oh what a slide!
With each twist and turn, we tumble with glee,
Squeals of delight echo, wild and free.

Strength grows in the giggles, the gasps, and the spins,
With every mishap, a chuckle begins.
Falling in circles, we stand back tall,
When life takes a spin, we can't help but stall!

A merry-go-round made of jests and cheer,
Gather your pals, hold your humor near.
The ups and the downs, they make quite a show,
A circus of laughter, come join in the flow!

So hold on tight, as we dance through delight,
In this spiral of joy, we'll soar like a kite.
With laughter as magic, our hearts interlace,
Through moments of fun, we find our true place!

Unyielding Saplings

We bend and twist, not break in half,
A sapling's dance, a little laugh.
With every storm, we sway and play,
For joy is found in every fray.

Sunny days or gloomy skies,
We wear our frowns like a sweet disguise.
Roots reach deep for water's tease,
While leaves above do sway with ease.

A gusty wind may cause a spin,
But check our smiles, we wear a grin!
Each tumble brings a playful tale,
Life's a game and we'll prevail!

So if you trip, just laugh it off,
Like all good trees, we'll never scoff.
In nature's dance, we're wild and spry,
With humor as our wings to fly!

The Heart That Heals

In the game of life, we trip and fall,
But with a wink, we stand up tall.
Our humor stitched, a playful thread,
Keeps us bouncing, never dread.

A tender heart can take a hit,
And still break out in a funny skit.
It's the chuckle after tears that steer,
A heart that mends with smiles sincere.

So when the world feels far from bright,
We'll wear our laughter, a shield of light.
With every chuckle, we heal the pain,
Riding the sunshine, dancing in rain.

Let's gather 'round, with jokes to share,
For laughter blooms in the open air.
Hearts that heal, no need to conceal,
With every giggle, we start to feel!

Cultivating Hope Underground

Down below where no one looks,
We're plotting fun like crafty cooks.
With trowels and smiles, we dig and play,
Planting seeds for a brighter day.

While topside folks, they march and strive,
We're in the dirt, feeling alive!
Each little sprout a hopeful cheer,
Bubbling laughter in the atmosphere.

Compost heaps and worms that squirm,
Make for jokes that twist and turn.
We're cultivating dreams so bold,
With plots and plants, new stories unfold.

From darkness sprouts a lively tune,
As we dance with roots beneath the moon.
We'll be the laughter under ground,
Growing fun where hope is found!

Shadows of the Past

With a wink and a nod, we stroll back in time,
To shadows dancing, oh so sublime.
A past that lurks with giggles and sighs,
In the corners where old laughter lies.

We trip over memories, pots of gold,
Tales of mishaps that never get old.
The mischief winks from the corners near,
With every glance, we find more cheer.

We'll tug on the threads of yesteryear,
Spinning yarns that bring us near.
For shadows can't cloud the joy we make,
Turning mishaps into a funny quake.

So here's to the past, the silly delight,
Where every blunder takes joyful flight.
We'll dance in the echoes of laughter's refrain,
In the shadows, we celebrate joy and pain!

Lights of Tomorrow

Up ahead, the lights brightly gleam,
An invitation, like a sweet dream.
With laughter leading, we venture forth,
To sprinkle joy, like stars in the north.

Each step we take, a giggle shared,
Mapping out futures that we've declared.
In every twinkle, a spark of glee,
The lights of tomorrow set us free.

Through valleys of doubt, we skip and trot,
Finding magic even in the not.
With humor guiding each joyful sway,
The lights lead us on our wondrous way.

So here's to tomorrow, so bright and bold,
Where laughter's the treasure more precious than gold.
We'll embrace the new with a chuckle and cheer,
In the dance of tomorrow, we'll spread good cheer!

The Undying Flame

In the kitchen, chaos reigns,
Spilled flour, and silly gains.
A toast to burnt toast, oh what a sight,
Chefs in aprons, a culinary fright!

But laughter keeps the spirits high,
As smoke alarms begin to cry.
We dance around with pots in hand,
A food fight? Oh, isn't it grand!

The flames that flicker, the flames that flare,
A pizza that's stuck, oh what a scare!
Yet in the mess, we find delight,
And swear we'll cook, not just ignite.

So here's to meals that go askew,
A lesson learned in every stew.
Life's little blunders, we can't outrun,
With humor in heart, we've already won!

Hope's Resilient Melody

A kazoo parade in the park we make,
With rhythm so silly, the ground will shake.
As squirrels join in with acorn drum,
Even the ants go, 'Here we come!'

Sing off-key, yes, that's our style,
A chorus of giggles that stretches a mile.
For every flat note or falter made,
We pull a face, and the troubles fade.

Hiccups and snorts, we sing with glee,
As birds look down, 'What's wrong with thee?'
But deep in the melody, we find our place,
In laughter and love, we triumph with grace.

So let's clang and bang like we own the show,
With every off-note, our spirits will grow.
In this wacky symphony so brightly played,
We hold the world close, not afraid!

Threads of the Untamed

A tapestry woven of socks gone rogue,
Lost in a dryer, oh what a vogue!
The mismatched pairs tell tales anew,
Of adventures taken, and laughter too.

With crayons in hand and walls as canvases,
Masterpieces bloom in messy advantages.
We scribble the skies and scribble the trees,
Our art says, 'Yeah! We've got the keys!'

In play-dough dinners and gooey pies,
We sprinkle the joy in each childlike surprise.
Our hearts are the needles, the love is the thread,
Together we stitch, no worries or dread.

So come, paint with whimsy, let's create a scene,
Where silliness reigns, and we're ever so keen.
In this wild, wondrous quilt, we find our way,
With every little thread, we brighten the day!

The Phoenix's Ascent

In the garden, butterflies work a show,
As I trip on a rake, oh no, oh no!
With flowers all giggling and blooms in a spin,
This clumsy gardener can't help but grin.

A sprout that wiggles, a pot that leaps,
A cactus that dances, oh, what a heap!
With petals on my head, I twirl in delight,
Each bloom a puppet, each bud a slight.

When the sun sets low, and the moon gets bright,
Even rocks can roll with pure delight.
With every tumble, we rise up tall,
Like a phoenix in bloom, we won't fear the fall.

So here's to the quirks, and the silly delight,
In the garden of joy, we take our flight.
For every stumbler who finds their wings,
Let laughter uplift us, and joy's song sings!

Gentle Warriors

In a field of daisies, we dance and sway,
With socks mismatched, we seize the day.
Mighty like a beetle, we'll take our stand,
With marshmallow shields, oh, isn't life grand?

We juggle our worries with pies in the air,
With giggles and chuckles, no room for despair.
Wearing armor of paper, our hearts are so light,
We fight the good fight with laughter in sight!

When storms come a-knocking, we're ready to cheer,
Our punchlines like thunder, there's nothing to fear.
With capes made of bath towels, we're ready to soar,
In this wacky world, we always want more!

So here's to the gentle, the silly, the brave,
With hearts full of mischief, we're ready to wave.
Through giggles and joy, we'll conquer the fray,
In this grand circus, come join us and play!

From Shadows to Light

In the darkest of corners, we dance like a spark,
With glitter and giggles, we brighten the dark.
We'll trip over shadows and laugh till we fall,
With banana peels flying, we'll conquer it all!

We chase down our fears like they're bad karaoke,
Singing off-key, it feels rather spicy.
When the sun starts to rise, we put on our hats,
With capes made of dusters, we're whimsical brats!

Our past might be messy, a slapstick affair,
But we paint it with joy, our hearts free to share.
Through puddles of laughter, we leap and we glide,
From shadows emerging, we do so with pride!

So gather, my friends, let's toast to the night,
With marshmallows roasting, our future is bright.
With humor and heart, we'll chase after dreams,
Turning shadows to laughter, or so it seems!

Embraced by Adversity

When life serves up lemons, we get out the cake,
With frosting and sprinkles, it's joy that we make.
Through hiccups and stumbles, we'll giggle and play,
In this dance of misfortune, let's swing the day!

Adversity's blanket may seem rather tight,
We snuggle up cozy, finding warmth in the night.
With pillows for armor, we bounce off the wall,
Our laughter is weightless, we'll never take a fall!

We juggle our troubles like clowns at the fair,
With pies in the face, but we don't really care.
Embracing the chaos, our spirits run free,
We twirl in the mayhem—oh, what a spree!

So raise up your glasses, let's toast to the grind,
With humor as fuel, we'll leave doubts behind.
Through tickles and laughs, we'll prevail and see,
That life's a wild party; come join in with glee!

The Tree that Bends

There's a tree in the yard, it sways with a grin,
With leaves in the breeze, it's just full of whim.
Like a jolly old giant, it dances with cheer,
While squirrels play tag, it giggles, my dear!

Against mighty winds, it does the limbo,
With branches all wobbly, it steals the show.
It knows how to sway, knows how to bend,
Through storms and rain, it will laugh till the end!

With roots underground, it's silly but wise,
It whispers to flowers, "Let's reach for the skies!"
In moments of chaos, it plays peek-a-boo,
This tree stands its ground while it jigs with the blue!

So let's be like the tree, young and unbent,
With hearts full of laughter, let's rise and attempt.
Through joys and the struggles, let's wiggle and dance,
For life's a grand show, so let's take a chance!

The Bridge Between

In the land of oddball ducks,
They waddled with their socks untied.
Each quack a bridge, through muck and plucks,
As laughter spread, they never sighed.

With each twist of fate, they'd giggle,
Dancing under cloudy skies.
If one would trip, the rest would wiggle,
In silliness, they'd always rise.

The bridge made of shenanigans,
Held firm by the joy they'd share.
Through muddy puddles and simple plans,
They'd float like feathers in the air.

So next time life throws you a curve,
Just grab some friends, and take a dive.
In every stumble, there's a swerve,
That keeps our inner giggles alive.

Echo of the Unseen

In a world of socks that don't match,
Lies secrets known only to the cat.
Each whiff of tuna, a sly little hatch,
Echoes of mischief where laughter sat.

With whispers of ghosts who prance with glee,
They tickle the toes of the old oak tree.
Invisible pranks, oh what a spree,
In the laughter's ripple, we all feel free.

When life gets heavy, the shadows pretend,
To drop silly jests from the sky.
Each giggle a note, a melodious blend,
Of humor that teaches us how to fly.

So hush now, listen, and just let it flow,
The echoes of joy are what we need.
In the unseen laughter, we learn to grow,
Planting delight is our greatest creed.

Soaring Beyond Storms

When clouds gather round, what a sight to see,
A flock of birds on a jellybean spree.
With each flap of wings, there's glee in the breeze,
They soar through the raindrops like runaway keys.

The thunder may rumble, the winds may moan,
But up in the sky, they've made it their throne.
With silly hats worn, their laughter has grown,
Through tempests of life, they've merrily flown.

For every droplet that tries to weigh down,
They bounce like balloons, no reason to frown.
In puddles they splash, in joy they abound,
As storms turn to giggles, they circle the town.

So if you hear thunder, don't run and hide,
Just grab your balloon and dance with the tide.
In the winds of mischief, let laughter be your guide,
Soaring through storms, we'll find joy inside.

A Path Through Shadows

In the garden of giggles with shadows that play,
Little critters sneak giggles, come out, don't delay.
They tiptoe on petals, come what may,
With chuckles entwined in a playful ballet.

Through darkness of night, they find the delight,
With firefly lanterns to brighten the sight.
Every whispering breeze brings surprising insight,
In corridors of giggles, they dance until light.

With a hop and a skip, they jump through the gloom,
Finding joy in the whispers, no place for doom.
Each shadow a sprout, where laughter can bloom,
In this playful path, there's always more room.

So whenever you roam, don't fear what you see,
Let shadows be friends, join hands in glee.
In every dark corner, find joy's decree,
On a path made for laughter, forever be free.

Stones that Shape Us

In the garden of life, we stumble and fall,
Each stone a reminder, we learn to stand tall.
With a wink and a chuckle, we dance on the rocks,
Life's had its giggles, like two silly fox.

We trip on our dreams, and sometimes on air,
Yet we wiggle with laughter, pretending we care.
The boulders are funny, like jokes in the sun,
They teach us to grin while we laugh and we run.

Life throws us pebbles, and we make a show,
Juggling our worries, just watch how we glow!
With each little stumble, we're crafting a tale,
Full of ups and downs, like a wacky email.

So let's gather our stones in a hilarious heap,
They shape who we are, as we jump and we leap.
With giggles and grins, we embrace the unknown,
For in this great quirk, we have truly grown!

Harvest of Strength

In fields of odd veggies, we learn to adapt,
Tomatoes with mustaches, it's laughter, not frapped.
With carrots in tutus, we strut like we're proud,
Our harvest of strength, in a jolly crowd.

Through storms of bad weather, we dance with delight,
With radishes giggling, we stay up all night.
The corn gives us wisdom, as tall as can be,
While peas crack their jokes, tickling the spree.

A funny farm festival, we throw every year,
With pumpkins on tricycles, we banish all fear.
With laughter the currency, we trade all our woes,
In this quirky harvest, true strength really grows.

So let's plant our dreams in this silly parade,
With humor our anchor, we'll never degrade.
We'll gather together, with veggies and cheer,
Creating our bounty, through laughter sincere!

Resilient Gardens

In gardens of giggles, we cultivate smiles,
With daisies in tutus, we dance down the aisles.
The weeds are there laughing, we pull them in jest,
For every green challenge, we know we're the best.

The flowers all chuckle, they sway in the breeze,
While bumblebees buzz in their silly trapeze.
We water with kindness and sprinkle with fun,
In this patch of delight, we'll bloom in the sun.

Our veggies hold secrets, they whisper in glee,
While cucumbers gossip, like best friends, you see.
With rakes made of giggles and shovels of cheer,
We nurture our gardens, there's nothing to fear.

So let's dig into laughter, it's rich and profound,
In this playground of nature, true joy shall abound.
With petals and punchlines, we grow ever bold,
In our resilient gardens, bright stories unfold!

Anchors in the Storm

When winds start to howl and the clouds start to frown,
We gather like anchors, not letting us drown.
With raincoats of laughter and boots made of cheer,
We dance in the downpour, with nary a fear.

The thunder's a drummer, the lightning a show,
We shimmy and shake, let the good times flow.
With friends by our side, we'll brave any squall,
In this circus of weather, we'll have ourselves a ball.

The waves may be crashing, the skies all a-whirl,
Yet we twirl in the tempest, each laugh is a pearl.
For in every sprinkle, there's joy to be found,
As we anchor together, we'll always stand proud.

So let storms come a-knockin', we'll greet them with glee,

For laughter's our lifebuoy, afloat like a tree.
With merry hearts open, we weather the plight,
In the anchor of humor, we shine ever bright!

Deep Waters

In the puddle, I took a dive,
My shoes floated, I felt alive.
A fish swam by with a grin so wide,
"You'll need a boat, not just your pride!"

But I just splashed, giggled, and twirled,
A fishy dance with the wet world.
The waves hit hard, my hair a mess,
Yet here I stand, just feeling blessed.

Strong Currents

Tossed by life like a paper boat,
I drift, I sway, and I gloat.
The current's strong, my snacks are few,
But my smile's bigger than the ocean blue.

"I'll row with spoons," I bravely told,
While my pals just chuckled, and gave me gold.
And though the storms come with a fright,
I paddle on, it's a silly sight!

Quiet Fortitude

In silence deep, I buy my time,
While squirrels plot and dance in rhyme.
I sip my tea, hold my comical frown,
Wisdom grows in this quiet town.

A tortoise passed with a wink and wave,
"Slow and steady, that's how we brave!"
With every sip and every sigh,
I'm the calm crow that learns to fly.

A Garden of Grit

In my garden, weeds do waltz,
I laugh and pull, but they have their faults.
The sun's too bright, the blooms too bold,
Yet laughter's worth much more than gold.

I planted seeds with promise bright,
But they grew ears, not flowers in sight.
Still, I smile at this patch of cheer,
For laughter's harvest is always near.

The Dance of Perseverance

I moonwalk through my daily grind,
With clumsy steps, and peace of mind.
The fridge hums a supportive beat,
While I cha-cha over leftover meat.

With every trip and tumble down,
I burst into giggles, chase away the frown.
So here I dance, with socks mismatched,
For life's a party, and I'm well-hatched!

Withstanding the Tempest

When life's like a stormy sea,
You just grab an old tree.
Dance through the lightning's flash,
And hope it won't make a splash.

Winds may huff and winds may puff,
Sailing through is never tough.
With a grin, I take my chance,
Call it my thunderous dance!

So even when clouds start to pout,
I don't fret, I twirl about.
With a quip and a clever jest,
I find laughter in this quest.

Should the rain drench my best shoes,
I just splash in joyous blues.
Mother Nature has her fun,
But I'm the one who's won!

Forge of the Brave

In the furnace of life's grill,
I heat my dreams with sheer will.
Charcoal thoughts, but coal's on fire,
A knight who dances on the wire!

The anvil rings with laughter's song,
While worries prance like they belong.
With humor sharp, my blade takes shape,
In every laugh, there's a great escape.

Turn the heat, don't just survive,
In this forge, I learn to thrive.
With a metal heart and jokes that gleam,
I'm crafting my extraordinary dream!

Every stumble, every fall,
Becomes a part of my bouncy ball.
In the forge, I smile wide,
With bravery as my joyful guide!

The Fable of Survival

Once upon a cheeky tale,
Of a cat who learned to sail.
Stormy seas, a fishy grin,
Made waves with his furry kin!

His boat was made of tinfoil hats,
As he outsmarted all the rats.
With a wink, he'd take the plunge,
Turning chaos into a sponge!

The ocean laughed, it rolled with glee,
As the cat pursued a life so free.
Jokes flew like seagulls in the sky,
For every fail, he'd still just try!

So if you feel you've met your fate,
Just remember, it's never too late.
Wear your quirks like a fancy cape,
In this fable, you're the escape!

In the Sweetness of Struggle

Life's a pie—sometimes it burns,
But who really ever learns?
Stir in giggles, add some spice,
Each mishap is a treat so nice!

Flour clouds when I knead the dough,
My kitchen skills are quite a show!
Yet every laugh becomes a crumb,
In sweetness, I find where I'm from.

Mixing ups and down's delight,
While frosting fails make cupcakes bright.
With sprinkles on my messy fate,
This struggle just tastes great!

So when the whisk starts to fly,
And the batter tries to say goodbye,
I'll whip up joy, put on a grin,
In this sweetness, I will win!

www.ingramcontent.com/pod-product-compliance
Lightning Source LLC
Chambersburg PA
CBHW051656160426
43209CB00004B/926